C. Hopkins

The Watchmaker's and Jeweler's Handbook

C. Hopkins

The Watchmaker's and Jeweler's Handbook

ISBN/EAN: 9783743418516

Manufactured in Europe, USA, Canada, Australia, Japa

Cover: Foto ©Andreas Hilbeck / pixelio.de

Manufactured and distributed by brebook publishing software
(www.brebook.com)

C. Hopkins

The Watchmaker's and Jeweler's Handbook

CHRISTMAS CHIMES

AND

OTHER POEMS.

BY

JULIA M. SWIFT.

PHILADELPHIA:
CLAXTON, REMSEN & HAFFELFINGER.
624, 626, & 628 MARKET STREET.
1877.

TO

MY UNCLE

Mʀ. GERALDUS T. STOCKDALE,

𝔗𝔥𝔦𝔰 𝔏𝔦𝔱𝔱𝔩𝔢 𝔅𝔬𝔬𝔨

ɪs

AFFECTIONATELY INSCRIBED.

CONTENTS.

	PAGE
CHRISTMAS CHIMES	5
KRISS KRINGLE	6
THE CHRISTMAS GIFT	9
LITTLE MATTIE'S DREAM	11
LITTLE SALLIE'S CHRISTMAS	18
THE OLD DOLL	21
HAPPY NEW YEAR	23
TOAST TO NEW YEAR	24
SLEIGHING GLEE	25
DASHING O'ER THE FROZEN SNOW	26
MERRY SLEIGH-BELLS	27
MERRY BELLS ARE CHIMING	28
CHRISTMAS ANTHEM	29
THE CHILDREN	30
WOMAN'S MISSION	32

	PAGE
The Separation	34
Disappointment	37
Fifty Years Ago	39
The Rescued Kittens	41
Our Mary	43
The Face at the Window	45
Twilight and Night	46
Grace	48
Somebody's Darling	51
The Tree and the Flower	52
Passé	53
Mother	54
Sweet Bonnie Louise	55
There's Beauty in the Twilight . .	56
Greeting to Spring	58
Come to the Greenwood Tree . . .	58
The Birdie's Song	60
Come Join our Merry Lay	61
Cuckoos are Singing	62
Sailing Song	63
Vacation Song	64
Kiss me, Mother, for my Strength is Gone .	66
No Longer Young	68

PAGE

CENTENNIAL ODE 71

OUT OF THE DARKNESS INTO THE LIGHT . . . 72

FREEDOM 75

THE ELM OF BUNKER HILL 76

RING THE BELL 80

SAD MOURNER 82

FACE TO FACE 83

BRING FLOWERS 84

IN MEMORIAM OF GEORGIE 85

TO MY SISTER IN HEAVEN 86

LITTLE DARLING, OPEN WIDE 88

LOOK UP 90

IN MEMORIAM OF HARRY 92

GREAT BETHEL 94

IN MEMORIAM OF MRS. E. G. 95

CHRISTMAS CHIMES,

AND OTHER POEMS.

CHRISTMAS CHIMES.

CHRISTMAS chimes, how sweet they ring!
   Tidings of great joy they bring,
Pealing on the midnight air,
Joy! salvation! everywhere.
The twinkling stars that shine so bright
Are smiling down in glad delight,
E'en as they smiled upon the earth
The evening of the Saviour's birth.

Humble shepherds heard and saw
The wondrous sight with fear and awe,

2

Let's hasten to adore, with them,
The lowly babe of Bethlehem.
And with the magi haste to bring
Fond " offering" to the Infant King,
All graciously He will receive
The very little thou canst give.

Then Christmas carols gladly sing
While Christmas chime bells sweetly ring.
Angelic choirs and seraphs bright
With us their golden harps unite ;
While heaven and earth unite to sing
The praises of the Infant King,
The joyous peal of Christmas bells
Upon the air in music swells.

KRISS KRINGLE.

'MID childhood's sweetest pleasures,
   Which memory fondly treasures,
     Are visions bright
     Of glad delight
And happy thoughts that mingle
With visions of Kriss Kringle.

Anticipations charming,
Fears somewhat alarming,
            They list to hear
            Those eight reindeer
And sleigh-bells merry jingle,
That hail dear old Kriss Kringle.

The stockings are hung so joyful,
In hopes to see them toyfull,
            With tops and balls
            And waxen dolls,
And luscious sweets to mingle
The gifts of old Kriss Kringle.

Then off to bed retreating,
With hearts quite loudly beating,
            They list the hoof
            Upon the roof,
And reindeer's names that mingle
With the shouts of old Kriss Kringle.

As midnight hour advances,
What bright expectant glances
            Are cast, so sly,
            With watchful eye,
Towards the fireside ingle,
With hope to see Kriss Kringle.

At every sound they hear him,
And wonder if they'd fear him,
    With eyes so bright
    And beard so white!
Yet pulses fairly tingle
At thought to see Kriss Kringle.

Yet soon each bright eye closes,
Each little form reposes
    So snug in bed,
    While through each head
What joyful visions mingle
With dreams of old Kriss Kringle!

And long before the dawning
Glad shouts hail Christmas morning!
    With mirth and glee
    They rush to see
The toys and sweets that mingle
The gifts of old Kriss Kringle.

Thus memory loves repeating
Those childish joys so fleeting,
    And old hearts thrill
    Most fondly still
As thoughts of childhood mingle
With memories of Kriss Kringle.

For who does not remember
The bright and gay December,
 With Christmas tree
 And jollity
Around the fireside ingle,
While greeting old Kriss Kringle.

Jovial old Kriss Kringle,
Merry old Kriss Kringle,
 With famous pack
 Upon his back,
And sleigh-bells' jolly jingle,
We think of old Kriss Kringle.

THE CHRISTMAS GIFT.

'TWAS Christmas eve; two curly heads
 Were nestled snug in downy beds,
Four blue eyes, so round and bright,
Were peeping over the coverlet white.
" Mamma" had kissed them and heard their prayers,
And " papa" carried them both up stairs;
For little "Ben" was only four,
And "sister May" but two years more.
Papa had told them to keep quite still,
And they'd see " old Kriss" the "stockings" fill;

Then gayly wishing them both good-night,
Left them to watch, in the pale moonlight,
The stockings, hung by the fireplace wide,
With a list of all the "wants" inside.
For "Ben" there were horses and guns and balls,
While "May" had ordered "dishes and dolls."

Suddenly May sprang out of bed,
And walking towards the chimney said,
"My dear old Kriss, I wish you'd bring,
I want it *most* of anything,
A *real live baby sister* here,
Won't you, Krissy? that's a dear!
And if you do, both Ben and I
Will be as good, as good as—pie!
Please don't forget, dear Kriss," she said,
Then quickly scampered back to bed;
And though they *tried* awake to keep,
The children soon were sound asleep.

'Tis Christmas morn! the stockings all
Are hanging full, against the wall,
With lovely candies, "games," and toys,
That charm the hearts of girls and boys;
But all unheeded, for they hear
A strange sound falling on the ear.
What can it be? 'tis not a cat,
Although it sounds somewhat like that;

They quickly rush, in glad delight,
To mamma's room, and *what* a sight!
The sweetest little babe, you'd think,
With velvet skin so soft and pink,
And oh! such locks of jetty hair
That gave it such a knowing air!
Its black eyes blinked at Ben and May,
In such a wise and funny way!
The little "pudgy" hands held out,
To say "howdo" to May, no doubt.
All breathlessly the children gazed,
For one short moment all amazed.
" 'Tis mine," said May, in proud delight,
"*I ordered it* from 'Kriss' last night;"
Then fondly murmured, as she kissed her,
" My Christmas gift! my baby sister!"

LITTLE MATTIE'S DREAM.

A CHRISTMAS STORY.

ON a little straw pallet, in fever so wild,
Was tossing and moaning, a poor little child.
Her head pained so badly she scarcely could see,
Her poor little hands as hot as could be.

In fever's embrace she had tossed thro' the night,
Her beautiful eyes so glassy and bright,
Her moans of distress were piteous to hear,
Piercing her mother's poor heart with despair.

'Twas Christmas eve, and many a shout
Of mirth and enjoyment rang merrily out;
And oh! what a contrast that jubilant din
Presents to the gloom and the sorrow within.

Long hours she had knelt by that little straw bed,
All hopeless and bitter the tears that she shed.
The child's plaintive wailings pierce through her
        soul;
Her terrible anguish she cannot control.

She prays to the Father of mercy to spare,
Or give her submission and patience to bear;
Then smooths the soft curls from her darling's hot
        brow,
Ah! surely she seems somewhat easier now.

O joy! her darling now peacefully sleeps,
And breathless with hope her vigil she keeps,
For hours and hours she watches each breath;
So faintly they flutter, oh! can it be death?

While thus she is watching in hopes and in fears,
I'll relate the events of the preceding years,

When peace and prosperity lavishly smiled,
And a fond husband watched over mother and child.

But five years ago she had such a bright home,
Ere her husband had left her the ocean to roam
In quest of more wealth for those dearly loved,
But alas! that sad voyage, how luckless it proved.

No letter, no message, not one little word,
From that fated vessel had ever been heard;
She was lost, but alas! none knew how or when,
For no one e'er heard of or saw her again.

The home and the furniture all, all were sold,
And soon the last dollar was painfully told,
For the bank that contained all their fortune had
      failed
Almost as soon as her husband had sailed.

Heart-broken and wretched she sought a new place,
And strove by hard labor the past to erase.
Yet all that she earned by her fingers was less
Than any one prosperous and happy could guess.

And now her loved Mattie, her one darling child,
Was struggling and raging with fever so wild.
She bent o'er the sleeper and wiped from her brow
The moisture so clammy that beaded it now.

For hours she watched thus the face of her child,
Till the sweet blue eyes opened and faintly she
    smiled;
What rapture! the little one knew her at last,
The critical moment so dreaded had passed.

A prayer of thanksgiving gushed forth from her
    heart,
And sweet, blissful tears refreshingly start,
As a radiant smile o'er the child's features came,
And faintly she murmurs her mother's dear name.

" O mamma, I've had such a beautiful dream,
I thought it was true, so real it seemed.
A beautiful lady, so sweet and so mild,
Stood close by my side; in her arms was a child."

" So charming, so lovely, too lovely for earth,
I knew that he must be of heavenly birth.
And oh, they were dressed in such beautiful clothes,
The same as they wear up in heaven, I s'pose.

" The beautiful child laid his hand on my brow,
So cool, so delightful, I 'most feel it now.
The sweet, lovely lady took hold of my hand,
And the fever all vanished as though I were fanned.

" Then she showed me a picture, oh mamma! so plain,
I saw our dear home and my papa again;

How splendid he looked, and how fondly he smiled,
And held out his arms to his poor little child.

"Then right in the midst of the room I could see—
Now, what do you think?—a Christmas tree,
All glittering with beautiful lights, I declare
For a while I did nothing but lie there and stare!

"Then when I turned back they had gone, mamma
    dear,
And no one but you, darling mother, were here."
The sweet voice grew fainter, again the child slept,
The mother in thankfulness silently wept.

A knock low and soft at the crazy old door,
A tall form is rapidly striding the floor.
For a moment she gazes in wildest alarms,
Then sinks all unconscious within the dear arms.

Joy seldom kills; her head she soon raised,
On the face of her husband so joyfully gazed.
"Oh! have you returned, then?" she wondering
    said;
"The sea has restored you, still living, not dead."

He told the sad tale of the terrible wreck,
Of the few who escaped from the fierce burning
    deck;
How they'd floated for days, till of hope most bereft,
One by one they had perished, he only was left.

Just as he thought he too must have died,
An outward-bound vessel the floating spar spied;
They bore him away to a far distant clime,
Where he lay in brain fever a very long time.

Since then he had searched for two terrible years,
Bouyed up by hopes, tormented by fears.
He had sought out the needy, relieved the distressed,
And gave ever freely the goods he possessed.

To-day he had gone on his usual round,
And, thanks be to God! his loved ones had found.
He had purchased their beautiful home o'er again,
For he felt that his search would not always be vain.

How fondly he gazed on his wife's lovely face,
And clasps her in tender and loving embrace;
Who could describe all those loving hearts felt,
As together by Mattie's hard pallet they knelt?

The mother then told of the wonderful dream,
Which more like a vision prophetic would seem,
Of the lady, the child, and the Christmas tree,
Which all realized they determined should be.

A carriage was brought, and a soft couch was made,
And on it the still sleeping Mattie was laid;
Overflowing with happiness swiftly they rode,
Leaving forever that wretched abode.

'Twas Christmas when Mattie next opened her eyes,
And gazed all around in bewildered surprise;
A lady stood near, oh who could she be?
So richly arrayed, so smiling is she.

Is she still dreaming? she gazes around,
Viewing the scene with amazement profound;
Just as she had dreamed, in the midst of the room
Stood a Christmas tree in luxuriant bloom.

'Twas gleaming with lights, and loaded with toys,
Such as fill little hearts with such exquisite joys.
She must be in heaven; she looks for her mother,
Behold! by the fair lady's side stood another.

A figure commanding, with fond smiling eyes,
She utters a cry of delighted surprise.
" O mamma! oh papa! it is, it *is* you;
My beautiful dream indeed has come true."

LITTLE SALLIE'S CHRISTMAS.

DOWN a court and through an alley,
　　Up a crazy pair of stairs
Dwelt a little child, named Sallie;
　　Poor and scant the garb she wears.
Little Sallie, only seven,
　　On the world's cold mercy thrown;
Mothers, think! oh, gracious heaven!
　　Just suppose it were your *own!*

Little Sallie still was grieving,
　　For her gentle mother died,
To the world her darling leaving—
　　To the world so hard, so wide.
But to trust in God she'd taught her,
　　And the dying mother's prayers
Beg that God will keep her daughter
　　From all worldly, sinful snares.

She had left a happy dwelling
　　For a husband, fondly loved;
But, alas! how sad the telling,
　　He had false and worthless proved.

Just one year ago he left her,
    Left her with her breaking heart,
Of all faith and hope bereft her,
    Worse than death 'twere *thus* to part.

Yet, for her darling had she striven
    Till tired nature sank at last,
And she left the earth for heaven,
    All her toils and sorrows past.
Little Sallie, thus forsaken,
    Wept and prayed with plaintive moan
That she might in heaven awaken,
    Please not leave her here alone!

All day long the child had wandered,
    Gazing at the Christmas toys,
Wondering at the money squandered
    By light-hearted girls and boys.
See, the snow is whirling lightly,
    Deep it lay upon the ground,
And the lights shine out so brightly,
    Merrily the sleigh-bells sound!

Hungry, weary, heavy hearted,
    Little Sallie creeps along,
For her wretched home she started
    Through the wind so keen and strong.

Sadly pinched each pretty feature
  Benumbed with cold are hands and feet,
Wearily the little creature,
  Trudges through each lighted street.

Timidly she asks a " penny;"
  Some scarcely hear her plaintive cry,
Others answer " have n't any,"
  All heedlessly they pass her by.
Yet the pitying angels guide her,
  Though earthly hearts are hard and cold,
Lovingly they walk beside her,
  With their wings of gleaming gold.

At length she reaches, oh, how weary !
  The wretched place she calls her " home,"
Gazes 'round the walls so dreary,
  Murmurs " Mamma, dear, I come."
'Tis Christmas morn, the joy bells ringing,
  Ringing out so loud and clear,
To the world " glad tidings" bringing,
  " Tidings" to all hearts so dear.

Stiff and cold the child is lying
  Dead upon the bare hard floor,
Ceased for e'er her plaintive crying,
  Safe upon the shining shore.

Child and mother both are singing
" Christmas anthems" of the blest ;
Little Sallie fondly clinging
To her loving mother's breast.

THE OLD DOLL.

YOU 'LL give me this lovely new dolly,
If I will consent to part
With my poor little worn-out Polly—
Why, ma'am, 't would break her heart.
How could I consent to leave her,
My darling I 've played with for years ?
Just see how your cruel words grieve her,
She 's actually shedding tears.

This grand-looking miss, so jolly,
With her velvets and ribbons and lace,
By the side of my poor little Polly,
Looks very much out of place.
For I must confess she is faded,
She 's met with so many hard raps,
No wonder she looks rather jaded,
You might yourself, perhaps.

3

She lost her sweet little nose
   By a thump against the door ;
And that hole in her head, I suppose,
   Was caused by a fall on the floor.
One beautiful eye was put out
   By a washing I gave her, one day,
But she sees with the other, no doubt,
   And hears every word that I say.

She lost all the hair from her head,
   Those lovely golden curls !
In a skirmish with cousin Fred ;
   He 's an awful torment to girls.
He held on with both his hands,
   And I pulled with all my might,
And when he let go—dear lands !
   But she was a terrible sight.

Then I made her some pretty lace caps,
   And trimmed them with 'cutest of bows,
So she looks most as well, perhaps,
   At least, till her hair again grows.
She's had every disease you could mention,
   And many a terrible fall ;
She required my utmost attention,
   I wonder she lived through it all.

But I love her more dearly than ever
For all her misfortunes, you see;
And never will part with her, never,
No matter how big I may be.
I would not forsake little " Polly,"
For all the new dolls you could bring;
For though they are handsome and jolly,
My darling 's a *different thing!*

HAPPY NEW YEAR.

HAPPY and light, happy and light,
Let us be merry and joyous to-night.
Banishing care, pleasure let 's share,
Gladness is everywhere.
Happy New Year, happy New Year,
Bring with thee blessings and bountiful cheer;
Sad hearts to lighten, dim eyes to brighten,
Happy, happy New Year!

Pledging a toast to those we love most,
Faithful in friendship shall e'er be our boast,
Wrongs we 'll forget, banish regret,
Trusting for happiness yet.

Cares of the mind fling to the wind,
Seek in the present enjoyment to find,
Warm greetings we send to foe and to friend,
Wishing them joys without end.

TOAST TO NEW YEAR.

HERE 'S a toast, here 's a toast to the happy
New Year,
And a parting salute to the old,
May it bring in its train every comfort and *cheer*,
And every blessing unfold.
May the dear ones we cherish prove constant and
true,
And loving hearts never grow cold.
May every blessing arrive with the New,
Every care disappear with the Old.

Here 's a toast, here 's a toast to the ones we love
best,
Whose smiles are so cherished and dear,
Through life may they ever be tranquilly blest
With many a happy New Year.
May the path they will tread be unclouded and
bright,
With radiant sunshine to cheer.
May virtue and truth ever guide them aright
Through many a happy New Year.

Here's a toast, here's a toast to the friends of
    mankind,
Who labor their good to secure,
Who teach them the pathway of virtue to find,
And aid them life's ills to endure.
Who sweetly console and relieve the distressed,
    Whose hand wipes away every tear,
May they and their dear ones be peacefully blessed
    With many a happy New Year!

SLEIGHING GLEE.

THE snow so white is gleaming bright,
    The sleigh-bells now are heard,
Then haste away in our dashing sleigh,
    We'll skim the earth as a bird.

O'er frozen rills and icy hills
    Away, away we bound,
The horses fly o'er snow-drifts high
    To sleigh-bells' merry sound.

The air is keen and fresh, I ween,
    But checks the brighter glow,
And dashing on with laugh and song,
    We skim the frozen snow.

Right merrily we sing our glee,
  Away with every care!
Sleigh-bells chime with the merry rhyme
  Upon the frosty air.

Our laugh rings out with merry shout,
  Our pulse with rapture thrills;
The horses bound to the sleigh-bells' sound,
  We heed not winter's chills.

DASHING O'ER THE FROZEN SNOW.

DASHING o'er the frozen snow,
    The moon is beaming brightly.
Cheeks like summer roses glow,
    Hearts are bounding lightly.
All our merry glees we sing,
    While the sleigh-bells' chiming,
As they gayly, sweetly ring,
    Mingles with our rhyming.

Nothing like a gay sleigh ride
    To banish care and sadness,
With the one we love beside,
    All is joy and gladness.

Laughing, singing as we go,
  Mirth and music mingle,
Dashing o'er the frozen snow,
  List! the sleigh-bells jingle.

Let 's be happy while we may,
  What 's the use of sighing?
Dashes on our cosy sleigh,
  Horses fairly flying.
While the music of the bells,
  With melodious ringing,
On the air so gayly swells,
  Mingles with our singing.

MERRY SLEIGH-BELLS.

O WON'T you go a sleighing? the sun 's shining
  bright,
And gayly 'tis playing on the snow gleaming white.
The sleigh-bells are ringing so merry and clear,
A sweet rapture bringing their music to hear.

The horses' hoofs are beating in time to our song,
As gayly we're fleeing so swiftly along.
Our pulses are tingling with pleasure and glee,
The sleigh-bells are jingling in sweet melody.

The snow gleams before us so dazzling and bright,
The sleigh-bells' sweet chorus our senses delight;
Now louder and clearer its melody swells,
O what can be dearer than the merry sleigh-bells?

The fleet steeds are bounding, our pleasure they
    share,
Our songs are resounding, we banish all care.
The sleigh-bells entrancing all music excels,
Our pleasure enhacing, oh sweet, merry bells!

MERRY BELLS ARE CHIMING.

MERRY bells are chiming,
    The festive time is here,
And youthful voices rhyming
    Corals to New Year.

Smiling faces meet us,
    Merry tones we hear;
Joyously they greet us
    With sweet words of cheer.

While the bells are ringing
    Gayly on the air,
Voices sweet are singing,
    Mirth is everywhere.

May the future find us
With our hearts as light,
Leaving care behind us,
Ever gay and bright.

CHRISTMAS ANTHEM.

REJOICE! rejoice! let all rejoice!
Again I say rejoice!
And let the praise of God be sung
By every human voice.

Angelic hosts and seraphs bright
Their voice and golden harps unite
To praise and magnify the Lord.
This night appeared, in flesh, the Word!

Behold! the skies are all ablaze!
In awe the lowly shepherds gaze,
Celestial music thrills the air,
Joy! salvation! everywhere.

Glory to God, to God on high!
To God! the echoes sweet reply,
And to good men on earth be peace
Which from this night shall never cease!

MISCELLANEOUS POEMS.

THE CHILDREN.

A FROLICSOME boy and two gentle girls,
    With bluest of eyes and brightest of curls,
Gladdened my life with the sunshine gay
Of their innocent prattle and merry play.
O, how I loved the music sweet,
The ceaseless patter of little feet,
Chasing each other out and in,
Filling the house with their merry din.

Never I wearied of questions asked,
Never I deemed myself o'ertasked,
As they ever came with some new demand
To claim the skill of my willing hand.
Dollies to dress, and toys to mend,
To many a game myself to lend.
Bruises to kiss, and stories to tell
Of dwarfs and giants and fairies as well.

Never a moment to call my own
Until the day's last hour had flown,
And three little darling curly heads
Were nestled snug in their downy beds;
Each little hand so dimpled and fair
Had been clasped as they knelt at their evening
     prayer,
The lashes closed o'er the eyes so bright,
As I blessed and kissed them all " good night."

So many years have passed away,
I look for the " children" in vain to-day;
For the baby boy I called "my own"
To manhood now has really grown.
The darling little chattering girls
Have " plaited up" their childish curls,
With all " young ladies' " airs and graces,
Of their childhood sweet the faintest traces.

Ah, yes! " the children" have surely fled,
Discarded each crib and tiny bed;
The " little ones" of " yesterday"
Have passed forever and ever away!
And oft as I sit in my home, so quiet,
I long for the romps and merry riot,
The childish laughter full of glee,
That can never more return to me.

O weary mothers, a word in your ears,
So swiftly pass the fleeting years,
A few will roll away, and then,
Behold the " children" are " women and men."
Then fill each childish heart with joy,
Not long they remain as " girl and boy ;"
Yet if their childhood bright appears
'Twill gild with light their after years.

WOMAN'S MISSION.

WHAT is woman's truest sphere?
    What her noblest mission here?
What her Heaven-appointed task?
What should woman be? I ask.
Must she in the rostrum stand,
The world to threaten and command?
Must she in the battle fight,
Where right is oft o'ercome by might?
Must she with the rabble mix
Deep in the mire of politics?
Must she for her rights contend—
Struggle fiercely to the end?
Must she with ambition soar
To heights that were unscaled before?

The world's much-dreaded censure brave—
Must she do this·or be a slave?
Crushed by man's despotic power,
Or prove the plaything of an hour;
His smile to court, his frown to fear,
Or wither 'neath the world's cold sneer?
Or must she be a butterfly—
To shrink in fear when storms are nigh,
Like other poor ephemeral things,
Lest they lose their gaudy wings;
Delighted to be deemed a belle,
And in gay toilettes all excel,
By minds as weak to envied be:
Is this fair woman's destiny?
Ah! no, methinks a high estate
Was here appointed woman's fate.
By deeds her usefulness to prove,
And sway the hearts of all by love.
Life's trials patiently to bear,
And others' joys and sorrows share.
To use her talents and her mind
To bless and benefit mankind.
With woman's intuition clear,
To see the false and the sincere.
By eloquence of word and pen
To elevate the thoughts of men.
By sympathy, her precious gift,
The weight from other hearts to lift,

To do, with all her woman's might,
Whatever judgment deems is right.
Her deepest influence be lent,
All sin and evil to prevent.
Her power in every rank of life
Be felt as mother, daughter, wife.
And, noblest mission *ever* given,
To train the little ones for heaven.

THE SEPARATION.

FARE thee well! 'tis better so,
    Better that we now should sever,
Than our aching hearts should know
    All that now they feel, forever.
'Tis vain, alas! 'tis all in vain,
    To hope for former joys returning,
To hope sweet peace will come again,
    For which our hearts have long been yearning.

Your once fond glance is now averted,
    And your brow is dark as doom,
Love his post has long deserted,
    Left us, shrouded thick with gloom.

How our love so strangely perished,
　　Changed to this o'erwhelming woe,
Love so long and fondly cherished,
　　Neither you nor I may know.

I myself deem not all blameless,
　　Yet my woman's heart rebelled
When you uttered words so shameless,
　　And my sweet dream was dispelled.
Once my heart with joy pulsated,
　　Fluttered like a cherished bird,
Seemed with blissful joy elated
　　When your well-known voice I heard.

Base suspicions, misconstruction,
　　Jealous fancies, satire keen,
These all proved poor love's destruction,
　　We allowed to come between.
Then ensued recrimination
　　And reproaches o'er and o'er,
'Till life seemed all desolation,
　　And the heart could bear no more.

Poor, poor heart! so very human!
　　And my spirit far from meek,
I resented, as a woman,
　　Bitter words I too would speak.

It *may* be, when we have parted,
   Peace may come to each again,
Though we wander lonely hearted,
   Yet will cease this bitter pain.

List! Love's funeral knell is ringing,
   For his spirit, crushed, has fled;
Vain to his senseless form all clinging,
   All is gone, for Love is dead.
Strew pale, withered flowers around him,
   Twine his brow with faded leaves,
Alas! it was not thus we found him;
   Pale Despair a chaplet weaves.

How our little ones will wonder
   When they hear the fatal news,
That our ties are rent asunder,
   And they must between us choose.
Yet, oh, God! I could not share them,
   How my heart writhes at the thought!
Then be merciful and spare them,
   Their sweet lives I've dearly bought.

I will ask no greater treasure,
   Never seek thy gold to share;
Wealth can bring the heart no pleasure
   When the cankering worm is there.

Could you find for them another,
  To supply to them my place?
Who so patient as a mother,
  Who her care could e'er replace?

Dark and cold the shadows o'er us,
  As our separate paths we tread;
Sad the future looms before us,
  For our mutual love is dead.
You, perhaps, may find another
  To whom you 'll give the *name* of wife,
But to the sacred cares of mother
  I devote my future life.

DISAPPOINTMENT.

THERE is a weight of anguish
  No tongue or pen can tell,
And only those who feel the sting
  Can understand it well.
'Tis cruel and relentless,
  With such a blighting power,
The brightest hopes e'er cherished,
  It withers in an hour.

In deepest gloom 'tis shrouded,
    Hope may not enter there,
But flees away in terror,
    Replaced by grim despair.
What is this power so fatal
    That lacerates the heart,
And all its quivering tendrils
    Tears ruthlessly apart.

The lip may still be smiling,
    The brow from furrows free,
Yet gnawing at the heart-strings
    This canker still may be.
No human skill availeth,
    No sympathy consoles,
And only God's sweet mercy
    Such agony controls.

The heart conceals its presence,
    Pride stands the sentinel,
With fiery sword uplifted,
    And guards the secret well.
What name has this fierce dragon,
    That thus can hearts devour,
And every sweet emotion,
    With such relentless power!

That blights the tender blossom
  With pestilential breath,
That dooms the full-blown flower
  To dark untimely death?
Its name is Disappointment,
  He rings the funeral knell
Of love and hope and happiness;
  He's known, alas, too well!

FIFTY YEARS AGO.

I DREAMED that we were young again,
    That we had wandered back,
And trod once more the flowery plain
  From off life's beaten track.
You were a boy in jacket short,
  And I a merry girl
With frock that oft in briers caught,
  And many a tangled curl.

The old brown school-house too I saw,
  The well-remembered birch
That kept us little ones in awe;
  The dear old whitewashed church,

Where through the window roses crept,
    The sunshine looked so gay,
All through the sermon old folks slept,
    And young ones used to play.

The orchard full of apple-trees,
    Where oft we went to swing;
The merry hum of busy bees,
    And each familiar thing;
The sparkling little meadow brook,
    Where hours we used to fish,
With crooked pin for fishing-hook,
    And burdock leaf for dish.

Thus fleeted by the happy hours
    In sport and merry play,
We revelled 'mid life's fairest flowers;
    It seems but yesterday.
We lived together side by side,
    Our sweet contented life,
'Till I became your loving bride,
    Your fond and faithful wife.

As on your altered form I gaze,
    And locks now snowy white,
I think of those delightful days
    When locks were dark and bright:

And yet our love more warmly glows,
  Increasing with our years;
As we grow weak it stronger grows;
  And ever young appears.

How many years have fleeted by
  Since those sweet days of yore,
And oft in thought I smile and sigh
  As memory calls them o'er.
For touchingly the heart will cling,
  Though heads be old and gray,
To every sweet familiar thing
  Of days long passed away.

THE RESCUED KITTENS.

A FACT.

" THOSE kittens *must* be drowned, I say;
    It shall be done this very day,
While yet they are too young to know
The fate they have to undergo.
'Tis all in vain for you to plead,
More cats than one we do not need."
In vain my eloquence I used
To save the kittens so abused,

For spite of all I said or urged,
I found the "kits" must be submerged.
Reluctantly I ceased to plead ;
They had *resolved* to do the deed.
The old " puss" 'neath the table sat
Listening to their *pleasant* chat,
And heard me pleading, all in vain,
Her little pussies' lives to gain.
Then sadly to my room I went,
My thought on watery deaths intend,
And drowning "kits" to meditate,
Leaving " kitties" to their fate.
While thinking of these sad affairs,
Methough I heard, upon the stairs,
A very odd, peculiar sound,
A thump, a jump, and then a bound,
A pause on every step, thump, thump,
In sprang the old cat with a jump!
And wondrous sight! who could have thought?
A kitten in her mouth she brought!
Upon my lap she sprang, and there
She laid her infant, young and fair.
Then down the stairs she fairly flew ;
I wondered what she next would do.
While sitting thus without a word,
The same peculiar sound I heard.
Again she came, and laid the other
Beside his little baby brother ;

Then rubbed her head against my knees,
And purred, as if to say, "Oh! please
My little darlings to protect,
Your kind assistance I expect."
I stroked her soft and glossy head,
My eyes suffused with tears, and said:
"My dear old puss, a friend you 've found;
Your little ones shall *not* be drowned,
For they shall be my special care,
And no one shall e'en hurt a hair."
And when the strange exploit I told,
No heart was found so hard and cold
To drown the kittens after that;
Each kitten lived to be a cat.
They sought to prove their grateful thanks
By many graceful, merry pranks;
And oft we 've laughed right merrily
Their frolics and their tricks to see.

OUR MARY.

DO you know our pretty Mary?
She dances like a fairy;
Her heart so fond and loving,
Its sweet affection proving.

Her ample brow disclosing
Grand thoughts are there reposing,
In that busy brain now teeming
With pretty baby scheming.

Her eyes, so dark and tender,
Like two bright stars in splendor,
Send many merry flashes
Beneath those silken lashes.

How " cute" her little nose is,
As it saucily reposes
Between the soft cheeks glowing,
Like roses richly blowing.

Her pouting lips, like cherries,
Or sweet delicious berries,
Seem only made for kisses,
And all love's joys and blisses.

This winsome little fairy.
Could never be contrary,
But sweet and loving ever,
And never naughty—never !

So full of fond caressing,
Papa's joy and mamma's blessing,
She wins our fond affection ;
We think her just perfection.

While to our hearts we press her,
We pray that God will bless her
With grace that ne 'er will vary,
Our bonnie little Mary !

THE FACE AT THE WINDOW.

I PASS, every day, a fine mansion,
   To see through the curtains of lace,
And damask silken hangings,
   A lovely childish face.
Glittering ringlets twining
   'Round the sweet angelic brow,
That seems like a halo shining;
   Methinks I see him now.

A far-away plaintive expression
   Dwells in those luminous eyes,
As though he were ever communing
   With forms far above the blue skies.
And daily I pass that mansion,
   To see through the window pane
That face, I oft linger to gaze at,
   And turn back to look again.

Through sunshine or storm I passed there
  At that self-same hour, to see
That beautiful face at the window
  That possesses such charms for me.
For it seems like a lovely cherub
  Through the beautiful curtains of lace;
And I long to press fondest of kisses
  On that beautiful baby face.

A week had elapsed ere I'd passed there;
  I gazed for that face in vain;
And I felt, with an inward foreboding,
  I should ne'er on earth see it again.
The white ribbons that streamed from the windows
  Plainly said I should see him no more;
But he smiles still more sweetly in heaven
  Than he smiled through the window of yore.

TWILIGHT AND NIGHT.

TWILIGHT shadows soft are stealing
  Over vale and mountain height,
Nature's glowing charms concealing,
  Gliding on to meet the night.

Weary nature longs to greet her,
    For the sun has gone to rest ;
E'en the balmy air is sweeter
    Springing from the golden west.

Hushed the scene, and calm and holy,
    For another day has gone.
Flowers bow their heads so lowly
    As the night comes gliding on.
Now, in all her radiant splendor,
    Smiles the lady moon so bright,
Myriad twinkling stars attend her,
    In honor of the queen of night.

Far above the tree-tops peeping,
    Flooding mountain vale and streams,
While the world below is sleeping,
    Wrapped in bright and happy dreams—
List! the nightingale is singing;
    How delicious are his notes!
To the air his rapture flinging,
    Softly sweet the echo floats.

GRACE.

HOW perfectly well I remember,
    Though so many years ago,
'Twas the very last day of December, ·
    The ground was covered with snow.
I sat by the fireside musing
    On all the events of the day,
A book now and then perusing
    In a desult'ry kind of a way.

The fire was cheerfully blazing,
    The flames leaping higher and higher,
As I sat there wistfully gazing
    In the depths of the beautiful fire.
A feeling of sadness possessed me,
    Long months I had bitterly wept,
For a beautiful angel had blessed me,
    But under the snow she now slept.

My heart was bitterly aching
    As I thought of that little form,
It seemed as though it were breaking,
    As I sat by the fireside warm.

The twilight shades were stealing,
  And all outside was gloom;
Inside the fire was revealing
  The comfort that reigned in the room.

As the blinds I was slightly raising
  To look on the scene outside,
I met two eyes wildly gazing
  With wonder opened wide.
One glance at the little creature,
  And I reassuring smiled,
For though pinched each pretty feature,
  'Twas a fair and lovely child.

I flew to the door and brought her
  In from the bitter cold;
So strangely shy, I thought her
  So prematurely old.
Her clothes were old and faded,
  Her shoes to tatters worn;
She looked so pinched and jaded,
  So wretched and forlorn.

Her story was soon related,
  No parents' care she 'd known,
A poor little outcast, fated
  On the world's cold alms to be thrown.

None had a right to claim her,
  She had no abiding place ;
I asked her what I should name her,
  She softly answered, Grace.

Soon she had food and raiment,
  The clothes my darling wore,
Her smiles of delight were payment,
  She thanked me o'er and o'er.
Soon her weary form was reposing
  In my darling's little bed,
In slumber the sweet eyes closing,
  Soft pillowed the tired head.

We took the poor waif as given
  Our loved one to replace,
And daily we thank kind Heaven
  For the gift of our precious Grace.
She has proved our dearest treasure,
  Our very hearts' delight,
Her goodness no words can measure,
  Our care did she well requite.

As to-night I sit here thinking
  Of all the happy past,
From thoughts of the morrow shrinking,
  While my tears are falling fast.

To-morrow her hand will be given,
  And her loving heart beside.
May he prize as a gift from heaven,
  His beautiful Grace, his bride.

♪ ————————

SOMEBODY'S DARLING.

HOW sweet to be somebody's darling,
  Let fortune frown black as she will,
The " Fates" and the " Furies" be snarling,
  For *some* one to cherish you still.
To feel that your coming e'er blesses,
  Your going leaves tender regret,
Who greets you with fondest caresses;
  What joy to be somebody's " pet"!

How sweet to be somebody's darling,
  To hear, in love's marvellous tone,
Sweet words of endearment, my " starling,"
  My " blessing," my " loved one," " my own."
To know that one fond heart is beating
  With warmest emotions for you,
Who meets you with tenderest greeting,
  Who 's constant and loving and true.

How sweet to be somebody's darling,
  Somebody's treasure and pride;
No matter how fate may be snarling,
  No matter what fortune betide.
To know you are somebody's pleasure,
  That your smile has a power to bless,
To whom you are life's dearest treasure,
  Beyond all the world could possess.

THE TREE AND THE FLOWER.

A TRANSLATION.

A LOFTY tree reared high his head,
    And stretched afar his sturdy arms,
Unto himself he proudly said,
  " How wondrous are my many charms!
For ages have I still defied
  The lightning flash, the tempest's power,
Unlike this flow'ret by my side,
  Who lives and blossoms one short hour."

While thus in haughty scorn he spoke,
  The sullen clouds had darkly lowered.
In wildest wrath the tempest woke,
  The lightning flashed, the thunder roared.

List! 'mid the din, a horrid crash!
  The tree is struck! 'tis rent in twain!
O never more in pride so rash
  The lordly tree may boast again.

Anon the sun in splendor shines,
  All nature sweetly smiles once more,
Beside the blighted tree still twines
  The flow'ret, lovelier than before.
More fragrant day by day she grew,
  Contented with her humble dower;
Ah! which is fairer now to view,
  The fallen tree or blooming flower?

PASSÉ.

WHAT is that great, mysterious change,
    Insidious, subtle, passing strange,
That leaves its stern relentless trace
Upon the fairest, loveliest face?
So imperceptibly it steals,
Its presence surely it reveals,
And seems in accents harsh to say,
Youthful charms I steal away.
Alas! I hear those mournful tones,
My face the dreaded presence owns,

5

And yet so stealthy its approach
I scarce could note its first encroach.
It is not that my charms have fled,
And youth's enchanting graces sped.
For see! my locks of silken jet
Are glossy and luxuriant yet.
The rose still blooms upon my cheek,
But oh! that voice doth loudly speak;
Each feature I have closely scanned
To note where this unsparing hand,
So ruthless in its every touch,
Has marred the beauty prized so much.
My teeth might still outrival pearls,
"A charm most highly prized by girls;"
And yet that *something* seems to say,
Youth has passed fore'er away.

MOTHER.

THERE is a fond and tender word
  Far dearer than all other,
By which the very heart is stirred—
  The holy name of mother.

That name will cause a deeper thrill
  Than father, sister, brother,
Awaking love more tender still,
  The love we bear our mother.

With many loves the heart may teem,
  It ne'er can know another
So pure, so constant, so serene,
  As that it feels for mother.

How sad the home without her care,
  How many griefs they smother,
How many heart-pangs those who share
  A home without a mother.

But oh! how bright the fireside seems
  To father, sister, brother,
When tenderly upon them beams
  The cheering smile of mother.

SWEET BONNIE LOUISE.

A SUNBEAM entrancing so joyously bright
  Little feet dancing in constant delight.
Never a sorrow or trouble has she,
Every morrow seems brighter to be.
Lovely and winning, e'er certain to please
Pure and unsinning, sweet bonnie "Louise."

Luxuriant tresses of glittering gold,
Seem in their meshes bright sunbeams to hold.

Eyes of dark splendor, brimful of glee,
Loving heart tender, from guile ever free.
With mirth overflowing, delighted to tease,
With happiness glowing, sweet " bonnie Louise."

All hearts fondly bless her, where'er she may be,
All long to caress her, so winning is she.
O never may sadness o'ercloud that fair brow,
But life smile with gladness as radiant as now.
To fond ones who love her, may she prove a heart's
    ease,
Till life's dream be over, sweet bonnie Louise.

* * *

THERE'S BEAUTY IN THE TWILIGHT.

THERE'S beauty in the twilight,
   At close of summer's day,
When clouds of gold and amber
   Have changed to quiet gray.
When all is still and tranquil,
   Except the whip-poor-will,
The sighing of the breezes,
   And murmur of the rill.

There 's beauty in the twilight
  When the sun has gone to rest,
And little birds are dreaming
  Within each downy nest.
A gentle, tender sadness
  Comes stealing o'er us then,
And visions long departed
  Come flitting back again.

The incense of the flowers
  Makes fragrant all the air,
The sweet delicious perfume
  Ascending like a prayer.
The heart communes with nature,
  And yields to her control,
And peaceful thoughts and holy
  Awaken in the soul.

There 's beauty in the twilight
  No other hour can know,
A sweet mysterious influence
  Pervading all below.
Enchanting dreams of beauty
  Awaken in the breast;
Ah! yes, the hour of twilight
  Is sweeter than the rest.

GREETING TO SPRING.

NATURE is rising from winter's embrace,
    Spring is surprising the world by her grace;
She touches the streamlets, bursts fetters in twain,
They dance on rejoicing in freedom again.
With dexterous fingers she dresses the trees,
Her balmy breath lingers and floats on the breeze,
With garments of verdure she robes all the earth,
And as she advances flowers spring into birth.
The birds serenade her in joyous refrain,
All gladly we hail her to greet us again.

COME TO THE GREENWOOD TREE.

COME, oh come, to the greenwood tree!
    Happy and gay, happy and gay!
Filling the woods with our melody,
    Merrily all the day.
Sweetly smiling the soft blue sky,
    Lovely and bright, lovely and bright;
Mirth is beaming in every eye,
    In every heart delight.

Gayly roaming the whole day long,
　　Joyous and free, joyous and free,
Merrily singing a happy song
　　Under the greenwood tree.
Banishing every trace of care,
　　Cheerily sing, cheerily sing,
Light and free as the summer air,
　　Or as a bird on the wing.

Twining garlands of wildwood flowers
　　Fresh as the morn, fresh as the morn,
Softly reclining in shady bowers,
　　Tresses we gayly adorn.
Gently the balmy summer breeze
　　Rustles along, rustles along;
Birds are trilling in greenwood trees,
　　Joining our happy song.

THE BIRDIE'S SONG.

TRA la, la, la; tra la, la, la, la, la, la!
    Listen to the birdie's song!
Tra la, la, la; tra la, la, la, la, la, la!
    It gayly floats along.
Ere the rosy glow of dawn
    Smiles with joy on vale and hill,
While the dew is fresh upon the lawn,
    You may hear my happy trill.
                    Tra la, la.

With joy I build my tiny nest,
    Not a grief or care have I,
With my loving mate I 'm sweetly blest,
    And I sing right merrily.
                    Tra la, la.

Very little is my need
    As I fly from tree to tree,
My birdies wee I daily feed,
    Then I trill with joy and glee.
                    Tra la, la.

When the sun has gone to rest,
　Fall the shadows of the night,
My birdies nestle 'neath my breast
　Till the rosy dawn of light.
　　　　　　　Tra la, la.

COME JOIN OUR MERRY LAY.

COME join our merry lay,
　Gladly we 'll sing to-day,
Singing the praise of May,
　Sweet, lovely May.

Now gloomy winter 's past,
Borne on the howling blast;
Sweet May has come at last,
　Sweet May at last.

See! at sweet May's advance
Gayly the streamlets dance,
Flashing the sun's bright glance,
　The sunbeam's glance.

List to the woodland notes
Warbled from tiny throats!
Sweet music gayly floats,
　Sweet music floats.

Gladly we 'll pass the hours
Culling sweet wild-wood flowers,
Blooming in mossy bowers,
    Sweet wild-wood flowers.

Banish all care and gloom,
See how the roses bloom,
Wafting their rich perfume,
    Wafting perfume.

CUCKOOS ARE SINGING.

BANISH all care away, let every heart be gay!
    Welcome the lovely May, welcome the lovely
        May.
Nature with fond delight welcomes her face so
        bright;
List, how the birds unite! list, how the birds unite!
            Cuckoos are singing,
            Glad tributes bringing,
            Woodlands are ringing
                Welcome to Spring!
        Cuckoo! cuckoo! sweetly they sing!
        Cuckoo! cuckoo! welcome fair Spring!

May decks with flowers again valley and hill and
    plain ;
Winter has ceased to reign! winter has ceased to
    reign!
Brightly the roses glow, gayly the waters flow,
Softly the zephyrs blow, softly the zephyrs blow.
       Cuckoos are singing,
       Glad tributes bringing,
       Woodlands are ringing
        Welcome to Spring.
    Cuckoo! cuckoo! sweetly they sing.

SAILING SONG.

COME sail with me o'er the heaving sea,
    Where the sparkling billows play,
We 'll lightly bound, to music's sound,
    Through the foaming ocean spray.
The waves smile bright in the glad sunlight
    With feathery foaming crest
As they play and leap, while the storms still sleep
    In the ocean's heaving breast.
Then sail with me o'er the bounding sea,
    O'er the foaming waters wide,
And we 'll lightly bound to music's sound,
    With the ever-surging tide.

Our hearts will bound as we list the sound
  Of the breakers' dash and roar;
Like the music grand of a mighty band,
  As they break against the shore.
We 'll swiftly glide o'er the billows wide
  And skim their feathery crest,
While the wind makes free with the brave old sea,
  And heaves his mighty breast.

VACATION SONG.

WITH voices light and gay
    We 'll sing a merry strain;
Vacation, happy day,
  Has come to us again.
To school good-bye awhile,
  For weary tasks are done,
All faces wear a smile,
  Vacation has begun.
    Vacation, happy time,
      We hail thee with delight,
    While every heart with pleasure beats,
    And every eye is bright.

We 'll seek a cool retreat
  Midst wood and groove so fair,
When birds make music sweet
  And balmy is the air.

We 'll wander all day long,
From every trouble free,
And sing a merry song
Beneath the greenwood tree.
Vacation, happy time.

Some climb the mountain-side,
And some will seek the shore,
To watch the rolling tide
And list the breakers' roar;
To sport 'mid ocean's foam
With shouts of mirth and glee,
All merrily will roam,
From tasks and studies free
Vacation, happy time.

Thus all will pleasure find
In sport and healthful plays,
And recreate the mind
The lovely summer days,
Until, vacation o'er,
To school we 'll all return,
Most cheerfully once more
All useful tasks to learn.
Vacation, happy time.

And now, dear friends, good-bye!
    We're parting for awhile,
And tears will fill the eye,
    Though lips may wear a smile.
May all enjoyment find,
    And meet with hearts as true,
Companions all so kind,
    And teachers, dear, adieu!
      Vacation, happy time.

KISS ME, MOTHER, FOR MY STRENGTH IS GONE.

AN INCIDENT OF THE LATE FLOOD.

"O KISS me, mother, for my strength is gone,
    The frightful waters surge above my head;
Long weary hours have I been holding on,
    And now the last remaining spark is fled."

Long, 'mid the fury of the tempest wild,
    They still had clung in desperation there;
The mother, powerless to aid her child,
    Now hears that wail of terrible despair.

The frightful flood had overflowed the land,
   The element no mortal power controlled,
And as she fled, her children by the hand,
   The furious billows high and higher rolled.

The mother's voice the little ones had cheered,
   Soon, soon would they a place of safety reach;
But see! O God! the bridge has disappeared!
   And terror seizes them, too deep for speech.

Yet to th' abutments, hopefully they cling,
   The boiling seething waters higher rise,
While through the appalling darkness fiercely ring
   The raging tempest's hoarse and sullen cries.

While o'er their shrinking forms the billows dash,
   And thunder in their terror stricken ears,
The frightful sound of breaking timbers crash
   Add still increasing horrors to their fears.

At last is heard that wild appealing cry,
   Which pierces through the mother's quivering
      heart,
" O mother, kiss me, kiss me once good-bye,
   My trembling fingers from their hold must part."

The child, whose strength had long been overtaxed,
   Her mother's quivering lips felt on her face;
The little trembling fingers then relaxed,
   She sank! the waters close and leave no trace.

The morrow came, all smiling is the sky,
  Serenely now the waves are gliding on,
Yet from their depths ascends that plaintive cry,
  "O kiss me, mother, for my strength is gone."

NO LONGER YOUNG.

NO longer young! no longer young!
    How sad the words appear,
When uttered by a careless tongue,
    And painful to the ear.
All harshly on the heart they fell,
    With new-awakened dread,
For ah! they seemed the funeral knell
    Of youth forever fled.

No longer young, how transient seems
    The rosy morn of life;
Replete with glowing happy dreams,
    With tender fancies rife.
The lovely dream dissolves too soon,
    And waking up at last
We find the morn has changed to noon,
    The bright hours fleeting fast.

No longer young, time's cruel pen
  Has marked the once smooth brow;
And on its snowy surface then,
  Are furrows stealing now.
The eyes have lost their laughing light,
  The rounded form its grace,
The cheeks that glowed with roses bright
  Now scarcely bear a trace.

No longer young, 'tis sad to think
  Sweet youth may not remain;
Each year is dropped another link
  From youth's bright golden chain.
Yet heart and mind *may* be arrayed
  In brighter charms than youth,
Which even time can never fade—
  Grace, gentleness, and truth.

No longer young! well, even yet,
  We need not idly mourn,
Or waste the hours in vain regret
  On what can ne'er return.
Let virtue shed her lustre bright,
  Old age she will adorn,
And with her brilliance make the night
  More lovely than the morn.
6

No longer young! yes, youth *must* fade,
  And rarest charms decay;
Yet charms in which the mind's arrayed
  Pass not so soon away.
Though eyes may be no longer bright,
  And locks may lose their gold,
The heart and mind a rarer light
  May every year unfold.

CENTENNIAL POEMS.

CENTENNIAL ODE.

A HUNDRED years have passed away
  Since first the great bell's pealing
Hailed Independence' natal-day,
  With new and solemn feeling.
When hearts were thrilled with joy profound,
  With great emotion shaken,
To see a nation at that sound
  To liberty awaken.

And loyal hearts must ever thrill
  With generous emulation,
The vows "our fathers" made fulfil
  To keep the declaration.
O heroes of the mighty past,
  Your spirit still is living,
For long as life and memory last,
  Our heart's best love we 're giving.

Then let each loyal heart awake,
  With joyful rapture thrilling,
In this triumphant song partake
  With heart and voices willing.
The dark and stormy days are o'er
  That blanch our cheeks in telling,
And to those heroes great, of yore,
  Our joyful song is swelling.

OUT OF THE DARKNESS INTO THE LIGHT.

RING out, all ye joy-bells of liberty, ring!
    Ye clarions and trumpets, ring merrily out.
Millions rejoice at the tidings ye bring,
    Rending the air with jubilant shout.
The long weary struggle for freedom is o'er,
So gallantly borne by the heroes of yore.
Hail to the dawning, farewell to the night!
Out of the darkness into the light!

Embalmed in all hearts are those memorable years,
    And each gallant deed of our forefathers lives,
The anguish endured, and the heart-scalding tears
    Of desolate sisters and mothers and wives.

To leave us, their children, their precious bequest,
They died, that with liberty we might be blest.
And freedom's fair form emerged, radiant and bright
Out of the darkness into the light.

When first they assembled, a congress to frame,
   What heroes composed it! what patriots brave!
All hail to each honored, illustrious name,
   Who freely gave *all*, their country to save.
Ne'er before met such a body of men,
So mighty with sword, with tongue, or with pen;
Their counsel directed the nation aright
Out of the darkness into the light.

Upon you, noble heroes and sages, depend
   The fate of a nation and millions to come.
O, will they their rights, so stupendous, defend?
   Or will they to Britain ignobly succumb?
Emotions are traced on the features of each,
Too deep for description, too mighty for speech.
Will they tamely submit? or gallantly fight
Out of the darkness into the light?

At length *Patrick Henry*, majestic and grand,
   Arises undaunted; what eloquence rolls
With all the great powers his heart could command,
   And surges resistlessly over their souls.

What pictures he draws of the slave's bitter fate,
How doth he on liberty's beauties dilate,
Till with one accord all voices unite,
Let us out of the darkness into the light !

What wondrous results, when Congress declared
    Their long-tried allegiance to Britain was o'er !
To fight for their new independence prepared,
    And sent the glad tidings from shore to shore.
The old State House bell rang its merriest peal,
Delighted the glorious news to reveal ;
And that fourth of July, a beacon star bright,
Arose from the darkness into the light.

What hardships they suffered, what perils endured,
    Delighted to follow where *Washington* led ;
To bitter privations most nobly inured,
    On the altar of freedom they gallantly bled.
They fought and they *conquered*, and freedom is
        ours,
With all its enjoyments and blessings and powers.
The star-spangled banner now floats in its might,
Out of the darkness into the light.

How lustrous the stars in that galaxy bright !
    Could heroes and sages so dauntless e'er fail ?
When names such as Hancock and Adams unite,
    When Jefferson, Lee, and a Rutledge we hail !

And many another one equally great,
Who wisely directed and governed the State ;
Determined the nation should rise in its might
Out of the darkness into the light!

Then ring! all ye joy-bells of liberty, ring!
　Ye clarions and trumpets ring merrily out,
For liberty's glorious centennial you bring,
　And voices respond with a jubilant shout.
A century even has floated away
Since that ever-memorable glorious day
Arose like a beacon star, radiant and bright,
Out of the darkness into the light.

FREEDOM.

WHILE Freedom was yet in her infancy
　　She charmed every loyal beholder;
She grew, in her grace and her beauty, to be
　Still lovelier as she grew older.
Her cradle was rocked by the bravest of men,
　Who kept o'er her vigils unceasing,
And for her their blood shed again and again,
　With faith and devotion increasing.

Brighter and fairer she grew every hour,
  Commanding the world's admiration;
For the fame of her beauty and wisdom and power
  Extends to each far-distant nation.
Everywhere true hearts respond to her call,
  Their vows of allegiance to render;
For her to conquor, or nobly to fall,
  Yielding their lives to defend her.

Chivalrous actions, performed in her name,
  The wonder of nations excited;
Her heroes are wreathed with the laurels of fame,
  Their faith and devotion requited.
Time but enhances her wonderful charms,
  Her blessings are freely extended;
Nations she 'd willingly clasp in her arms,
  Until all with fair Freedom are blended.

THE ELM OF BUNKER HILL.

THE brave old Elm-tree reared his head,
    Majestic, stately, grand,
As though unto himself he said,
  " In all this mighty land

There is not such another tree
  That can with me compare,
For many a thrilling history
  Is proudly written here.

" Yes, many a record of the past
  Is traced on every leaf,
In summer sun and winter blast,
  Of many a joy and grief.
My ancient, tawny trunk contains
  Full many a mystery,
Which in my inmost heart remains
  All unrevealed to be.

" When first my leafy branches spread
  And trembling shadows made,
How many a swarthy warrior's head
  Reclined beneath my shade.
And many a dusky maiden came
  To meet her hunter bold,
With eyes of light and cheeks of flame,
  To list the tale he told.
At length, one great eventful day,
  How much was I amazed!
When on strange forms in rich array
  And faces pale, I gazed!

They soon in strength and numbers grew,
  From o'er the ocean's foam
They came; and toiled with courage true
  To make themselves a home.

" What they endured 'twere vain to tell,
  Th' attempt my power shames;
The covert blow! the horrid yell!
  Their little homes in flames!
Yet still they persevered and throve,
  Still steadily increased;
Till westward far the foe they drove,
  And dwelt once more in peace.

"But soon oppression weighed them down,
  And trials great they bore,
Till they resolved that England's crown
  Should ne'er oppress them more.
Those dauntless hearts have much endured;
  For justice they contend;
Sweet liberty should be secured,
  Their rights they will defend.

" My every leaf doth thrill with pride
  The tale to tell again,
Of how those heroes fought and died,
  For freedom bravely slain.

Oh, if an aged tree could weep,
    My tears would freely flow,
At thought of those brave hearts that sleep,
    The gallant ones laid low!

" My aged eyes beheld a sight
    That every heart would thrill,
The fiercest and the bravest fight
    Just here, on Bunker Hill.
How furiously the conflict raged!
    A handful of brave men
With hosts of British foes engaged,
    Again and yet again!

" That time has past, I lived to see
    Sweet peace and plenty reign,
And smiling faces looked at me,
    While all was joy again.
The pealing chimes of freedom woke
    The echoes of the air,
They'd cast aside the British yoke,
    And joy was everywhere."

Thus rambled on the Elm-tree old,
    With all a veteran's pride;
Each leaf its tale of wonder told
    To all who stood beside.

And many a storm broke o'er his head,
  While oft the lightning flash
Struck other trees around him dead,
  That fell with horrid crash!

Yet stood unmoved the brave old tree,
  A record of the past;
But like all other veterans, he
  Succumbed to time at last.
To all he seemed a dear old friend,
  And all throughout the realm
Regretted much to see the end
  Of Boston's dear old Elm.

RING THE BELL.

WHEN first upon the air it pealed
  A hundred years ago,
What joy its iron tongue revealed
  To anxious hearts below!
The glorious tidings thrilled the air,
  Resounding far and wide,
The brave hearts throbbing proudly there
  Respond on every side.

The deeds our gallant sires performed
  On history's page we trace ;
Those deeds, that coldest hearts have warmed,
  No time can e'er efface.
May we, your sons, in time of need,
  Be e'er as leal and true
In every word and every deed
  For country dear, as you.

That bell the news so joyful told
  In tones so proud and strong,
Across Atlantic's waters rolled
  And echoed loud and long.
Then let the dear old bell once more
  Ring out a joyous chime,
And nations welcome to our shore
  From every distant clime.

IN MEMORIAM.

SAD MOURNER.

SAD mourner, why bitterly weeping?
  Why heaving with sorrow thy breast?
Thy loved one serenely is sleeping
  To wake in the home of the blest.
Life's wearisome journey is ended,
  All trials and conflicts are done,
" The angel of peace" has descended,
  And glory immortal is won.

O, weep not in sorrow despairing!
  Hope soothes thee with comforting voice;
Her pinions thy spirit up-bearing,
  Thy desolate heart will rejoice.
Bright faith, with her finger immortal,
  The beautiful gates will unfold,
And flinging wide open the portal,
  Thy loved one in glory behold!

Then put off the raiment of sadness,
    And list to the comforting word
That tells thee in accents of gladness
    'T is blessed to die in the Lord.
Soon, soon the beloved we must follow,
    The path to the tomb must be trod,
Then leave earthly pleasures so hollow,
    And meekly pass "under the rod."

FACE TO FACE.

LIST! the mournful sound of weeping
    Falling sadly on the ears,
For the loved one now is sleeping,
    All unmindful of our tears.
Hands together meekly folded
    On the now unheaving breast,
And the waxen features moulded
    In their everlasting rest.

O'er the quiet sleeper bending,
    Hearts are torn with cruel grief,
Yet amid their sorrow blending
    Comes a thought of sweet relief.
Though the precious form we 're leaving
    In the cold earth's last embrace,
Cease! oh, cease all useless grieving!
    She beholds God face to face.

Through this vale of shadows groping,
    Hearts would wither in despair,
Were it not the blissful hoping
    For a land more bright and fair.
This the promise sweetly cheering
    With a world of tender grace,
Though on earth the darkness fearing,
    Yet in heaven, face to face.

BRING FLOWERS.

BRING lilies and roses and fairest of flowers
    To garland her beautiful brow;
She's sleeping so calmly, this darling of ours,
    So sweetly and tranquilly now.
The little hands folded so meekly at rest,
    For life's weary journey is done.
How short was the way, how soon she is blest,
    So quickly the diadem won!

Then strew the pale lilies and roses around,
    Like to hers very brief is their bloom,
For soon they must wither beneath the cold ground,
    Yet how sweet is their lovely perfume!
She too was a flower exquisitely rare,
    Unfolding new beauties each hour;
Her sweetness and loveliness everywhere
    Exerting their magical power.

We grieve for the flower now faded and dead,
    So cold and so spotlessly white;
Its glorious beauty forever has fled,
    So lately our fondest delight.
Yet think not, ah, think not it bloometh no more!
    'T is only transplanted above;
More radiant still on that beautiful shore,
    Cherished by Infinite love.

IN MEMORIAM OF GEORGIE.

OUR darling is sleeping the sleep of the blest,
    Lilies and roses over his breast,
Dark silken lashes sweeping his cheek,
Hands linked together, folded so meek.
Soft hair brushed smoothly off the white brow,
Glorious eyes forever closed now.
Strew the pale lilies over his head,
Our darling is sleeping the sleep of the dead.

Could we behold him as now he appears
How soon would we banish all sorrow and tears,
Immortal and glorious, radiant and bright,
In that beautiful realm where God is the light.

    7

For a little while parted, but, blessed be God,
The path he has trodden by us shall be trod,
The strong hand unto him so lovingly given
Shall guide and direct us to Georgie in heaven!

Yes! fairest of flowers around him are spread,
Pale lilies and roses are wreathing his head,
Soon they must wither and lose their perfume,
But the crown he is wearing forever shall bloom.
O, heaven seems now more familiarly near
Since Georgie, *our* Georgie, our darling is there;
Sweet, sweet is the thought, for us he now waits
To meet us and greet us at heaven's bright gates.

TO MY SISTER IN HEAVEN.

SWEET angel sister! when thou wert on earth
    Methought I fully realized thy worth,
And understood the goodness of thy heart.
But, ah! 't was not till God had bid us part,
And crowned thy brow with immortality
I really knew all thou hadst been to me,
And felt the depth and sweetness of thy love
When never more its power I might prove.
Thy sympathy, so earnest, never failed,
No matter whether grief or joy prevailed,

That ever deemed thyself supremely blest
When joy and gladness reigned within my breast.
O loving heart, that with sweet joy was stirred,
When I, thy sister, was to thee preferred!
For selfishness to thee was e'er unknown,
And all sweet virtues marked thee for their own.
O tender eyes, that looked such love in mine,
E'er then thou wert less human than divine!
O, clinging arms, that twined in fond embrace!
O, lips that rained sweet kisses on my face!
All earthly joys I'd willingly resign
To feel again that sweet embrace of thine!
And though long weary years have passed away,
The need for thee grows stronger day by day.
Ah! couldst thou know all I have since endured
Thy spirit back to earth would be allured,
To give me o'er and o'er thy fond caress,
And my sad heart with consolation bless.
To press to mine thy soft and tender cheek,
And words of loving sympathy to speak.
Ah! oft I feel, sweet sister, thou art near,
And whispering loving counsel in my ear.
Thy sweet and gentle influence I feel,
And thoughts of peace and love around me steal.
I know thy loving prayers for me ascend
That I may persevere unto the end.
In heaven, darling sister, thou dost wait
To meet and greet me at the golden gate;

That when the brittle link of life is riven,
Thou wilt be *first* to welcome me in heaven.
Dear Lord! I thank thee for my sister's love,
O grant I e'er may worthy of it prove!
And, like to her, with sweet submission bend,
And, like to her, prove faithful to the end.

LITTLE DARLING, OPEN WIDE.

O LITTLE darling, open wide
　　The bright celestial portal,
Disclose the glory there inside
　　That clothes the soul immortal.
In all thy radiant charms appear
　　That unto thee are given,
To comfort sad hearts grieving here,
　　That thou hast gone to heaven.

O could they see thee as thou art,
　　In all thy heavenly splendor,
'Twould leave within each grieving heart
　　A peace most sweet and tender.
Thy little blossom blooms for thee
　　More lovely every hour,
From earthly blight and sorrow free
　　A sweet celestial flower.

Secure within the Saviour's arms,
   How fondly they enfold her!
All glowing with immortal charms
   In paradise behold her.
'Tis only for a little while
   That earthly ties are riven,
Soon shalt thou see her angel smile
   More lovely far in heaven.

Soon shalt thou gaze upon her face,
   No more in pain to sever,
Soon feel again her fond embrace,
   And claim her thine forever.
Above the azure clouds she waits,
   With fondest love to greet thee,
And through the glorious golden gates
   Looks joyously to meet thee.

O when a fragile little flower
   To heaven is transplanted,
We should rejoice His mighty power
   The gracious boon has granted.
For earth is cold and bleak and bare,
   And tender plants will perish;
But in His garden bright and fair
   He will preserve and cherish.

7*

LOOK UP.

TO ANNIE.

MY baby, oh! my baby,
  How can I let thee go,
And leave me here so lonely,
  So crushed with bitter woe?
How can I lay thy lovely form
  Within the cold, cold ground,
Where summer rains and winter storms
  Beat on the little mound?
Where never more thy baby lips
  My own may fondly press,
And never more thy winning smiles
  My heart may cheer and bless.
O thou art far too beautiful
  To lay beneath the sod;
But we must bow unto Thy will,
  And meekly kiss the rod.
Yet heaven has many angels,
  And I had only one,
O was it merciful, dear Lord,
  To leave me thus alone?

Be calm! repining spirit,
　　The Saviour knew thee best,
And took thy fond heart's treasure
　　To be forever blest.
'Tis true the earthly fetters
　　That bound thee, now are riven;
But ah, a dearer, stronger link,
　　Now draws thy heart to heaven.
Then cease thy bitter weeping,
　　Or weep not in despair,
And look *beyond* the grave-mound,
　　Thy darling is not there.
But crowned with bliss immortal,
　　Arrayed in angel charms,
She fondly waits thy coming,
　　Secure in Jesus' arms.
And when life's dream is over,
　　As soon, oh, soon 'twill be,
Thy little one will be thine own
　　For all eternity.

IN MEMORIAM OF HARRY.

INSCRIBED TO HIS MOTHER.

BRIGHT spirit of beauty immortal,
  Relentlessly torn from our love,
Thou hast crossed the mysterious portal
  That opens to mansions above.
How smiling thy young life is dawning
  With mental endowments so bright.
Oh, could we foresee such a morning
  Would change to such terrible night?

Ah! fond recollections are clinging
  To hopes far too brilliant to last,
And memory mournfully bringing
  Sweet joys that forever are past.
Thy childhood, that like a rare flower,
  New beauties would daily disclose,
Developing marvellous power,
  Alas! how untimely its close.

Oh, never again to behold thee!
  To gaze on thy soul-speaking face!
Oh, never again to enfold thee
  In tender maternal embrace!

Oh, never to look for thy meeting!
To listen all vainly to hear
Thy voice in its heart-cheering greeting,
So familiar and sweet to the ear.

For thee tears unwonted are falling
From eyes unaccustomed to weep,
And loved ones are fondly recalling
Memories lasting and deep.
A friend firm and steadfast they proved thee,
Thy sympathy true never failed.
What wonder they tenderly loved thee,
Or thy fate so untimely bewailed?

But see through the storm cloud appalling
A rainbow of promise appears;
In mercy the spirit enthralling,
Smiling through sorrowful tears.
What though earthly fetters are riven?
Faith and Hope the sad spirit sustain,
And whisper, thou 'lt meet him in heaven
In all his young beauty again.

GREAT BETHEL.

ALL have heard Great Bethel's story,
　　Of a nation's grief and pride,
When for country, freedom, glory,
　Fearlessly young Greble died.
Loving hearts were rent asunder
　When the mournful tidings came,
That Great Bethel's fatal thunder
　Had immortalized his name.

First upon the country's altar,
　Laying down his noble life,
With courage that could never falter
　'Mid the battle's raging strife.
Though many a hero's blood has dyed
　That shrine, since Bethel's fatal plain,
Of many hearts and homes the pride,
　Yet was he *first* for freedom slain.

Never heart more purely glowing
　With all feelings warm and true,
With sweet tenderness o'erflowing,
　Filled with manly impulse too.

Hearts bereaved will e'er bewail him,
　Tears of anguish dew his grave,
Yet a nation's love doth hail him—
　" Foremost of the cherished brave!"

IN MEMORIAM OF MRS. E. G.

INSCRIBED TO HER CHILDREN.

WHEN first we found ourselves bereft,
　That thou hadst all the children left,
That God our dearest joy had taken,
Of *all* we felt ourselves forsaken;
For *thou* the very centre seemed,
Of all we were, or hoped, or dreamed.
No happiness could be complete
Without *thy* sympathy, so sweet.
For joys increased an hundred fold
When to our darling mother told.
We took to thee each childish grief,
And never failed to find relief;
While in maturer years we came,
And found thy sympathy the same.
No trial overwhelming proved,
Sustained by thy maternal love;

And whether grief or joy prevailed,
Thy love, so tender, never failed.
Thou wert the sunshine of our lives,
Best of mothers, *best* of wives.
O language never can express
Thy magic power to soothe and bless!
And oh! what words could e'er reveal
The weary, aching void we feel?
The world itself seems wrapped in gloom,
The brightest place our mother's tomb.
In dreams the music of thy voice
Our hearts so desolate rejoice.
And only then, we feel the bliss,
The thrilling pressure of thy kiss.
O gates of heaven, open wide
That we may see her form inside;
That from the azure skies, so bright,
Her angel smile may cheer our night.
Sweet mother, see thy children's tears,
And listen to thy children's prayers;
O gain for us the grace, from God,
That we may meekly kiss the rod;
That when this weary life is done,
The crown of victory may be won.
What joy! what bliss! in heaven to be,
Dear mother, evermore with thee.

www.ingramcontent.com/pod-product-compliance
Lightning Source LLC
Chambersburg PA
CBHW032356280326
41935CB00008B/594